8-12

The new Solar System

Saturn

Robin Birch

CHELSEA CLUBHOUSE
An Imprint of Chelsea House Publishers

This edition published in 2008 in the United States of America by Chelsea Clubhouse, a division of Chelsea House Publishers.

Chelsea Clubhouse
An imprint of Chelsea House Publishers
132 West 31st Street
New York, NY 10001

Chelsea Clubhouse books are available at special discounts when purchased in bulk quantities for businesses, associations, institutions, or sales promotions. Please call our Special Sales Department in New York at (212) 967-8800 or (800) 322-8755.

You can find Chelsea Clubhouse on the World Wide Web at: http://www.chelseahouse.com

First published in 2004 by
MACMILLAN EDUCATION AUSTRALIA PTY LTD
15–19 Claremont Street, South Yarra, 3141

Visit our Web site at www.macmillan.com.au or go directly to www.macmillanlibrary.com.au

Associated companies and representatives throughout the world.

Library of Congress Cataloging-in-Publication Data

Birch, Robin.
    Saturn / Robin Birch. — 2nd ed.
    p. cm. — (The new solar system)
    Includes index.
    ISBN 978-1-60413-213-7
    1. Saturn (Planet) —Juvenile literature. I. Title.
    QB671.B57 2008
    523.46—dc22

                                    2007051540

Edited by Anna Fern
Text and cover design by Cristina Neri, Canary Graphic Design
Photo research by Legend Images
Illustrations by Melissa Webb, Noisypics

Printed in the United States of America

Acknowledgements
The author and publisher are grateful to the following for permission to reproduce copyright material:

Cover photograph of Saturn courtesy of Photodisc.

Art Archive, p. 5 (bottom); TSADO/Tom Stack/Auscape, p. 20; TSADO/NASA/Tom Stack/Auscape, p. 29 (right); Australian Picture Library/Corbis, p. 25 (top); Digital Vision, p. 26; Calvin J. Hamilton, pp. 7, 11, 22, 25 (centre & bottom); Walter Myers/www.arcadiastreet.com, p. 10; NASA and The Hubble Heritage Team, pp. 8, 9 (bottom); NASA/JPL, pp. 12, 13 (bottom), 24 (right); NASA/Kennedy Space Centre, p. 29 (left); NASA/NSSDC, pp. 5 (top), 21 (bottom); NASA/US Geological Survey, p. 23 (bottom); Photodisc, pp. 17, 28 (left); Photolibrary.com/SPL, pp. 4 (right), 6, 13 (top), 14 (bottom), 15, 19, 21 (top), 23 (top), 24 (left), 27, 28 (right).

Background and border images, including view of Saturn, courtesy of Photodisc.

While every care has been taken to trace and acknowledge copyright, the publisher offers their apologies for any accidental infringement where copyright has proved untraceable. Where the attempt has been unsuccessful, the publisher welcomes information that would redress the situation.

Please note
At the time of printing, the Internet addresses appearing in this book were correct. Owing to the dynamic nature of the Internet, however, we cannot guarantee that all these addresses will remain correct.

Contents

Glossary words

When you see a word printed in bold, **like this**, you can look up its meaning in the glossary on page 31.

Discovering Saturn

Saturn is a **planet** that looks like a **star** in the sky. Sometimes Saturn is bright, while at other times it does not stand out. People have known about Saturn since **ancient** times. It is the most faraway planet that we can see without a **telescope**.

The first person to look at Saturn with a telescope was the **astronomer** Galileo, in 1610. He had just started using a telescope he had made. Galileo was the first person to see Saturn's rings, but he did not understand what he was seeing.

▼ The evening sky, with (left to right) Jupiter, Venus, and Saturn

Saturn

▲ This is the symbol for Saturn.

In 1659, the Dutch astronomer Christiaan Huygens figured out that Saturn has rings around it.

The word "planet" means "wanderer." Stars always make the same pattern in the sky. Planets change their location in the sky, compared to the stars around them. This is why planets were called "wanderers."

▲ The planet Saturn

▶ The god Saturn (Cronos)

Saturn has at least 56 **moons**, eight of them large. The first moon to be discovered was Titan, in 1655. It was discovered by the astronomer Christiaan Huygens.

The first **space probe** to visit Saturn was *Pioneer 11*, in 1979. *Pioneer 11* took the first close-up pictures of Saturn.

Saturn was named after Saturn, the Roman god of agriculture. Saturn's name in Greek stories was Cronos. Cronos was the father of Zeus (Jupiter), and the son of the god Uranus. Saturn moves through the stars more slowly than Jupiter, so was named after the god Jupiter's father.

The Sixth Planet

The planet Saturn **revolves** around the Sun, along with seven other planets and many other bodies. The Sun, planets, and other bodies together are called the solar system. Saturn is the sixth planet from the Sun.

There are eight planets in the solar system. Mercury, Venus, Earth, and Mars are made of rock. They are the smallest planets, and are closest to the Sun. Jupiter, Saturn, Uranus, and Neptune are made mainly of **gas** and liquid. They are the largest planets, and are farthest from the Sun.

The solar system also has dwarf planets. The first three bodies to be called dwarf planets were Ceres, Pluto, and Eris. Ceres is an asteroid. Pluto and Eris are known as **trans-Neptunian objects**.

A planet is a body that:

- orbits the Sun
- is nearly round in shape
- has cleared the area around its orbit (its **gravity** is strong enough)

A dwarf planet is a body that:

- orbits the Sun
- is nearly round in shape
- has not cleared the area around its orbit
- is not a **moon**

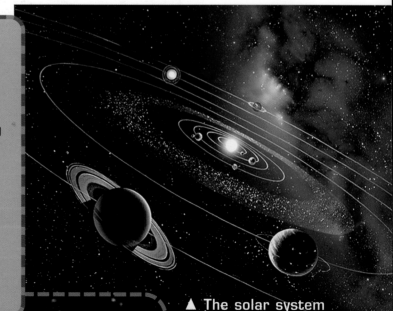

▲ The solar system

There are also many small solar system bodies in the solar system. These include asteroids, comets, trans-Neptunian objects, and other small bodies which have not been called dwarf planets.

Asteroids are made of rock. Most of them orbit the Sun in a path called the asteroid belt, between the orbits of Mars and Jupiter. Comets are made mainly of ice and rock. When their orbits bring them close to the Sun, comets grow a tail. Trans-Neptunian objects are icy, and orbit the Sun farther out on average than Neptune.

▶ The eight planets are Mercury, Venus, Earth, Mars, Jupiter, Saturn, Uranus, and Neptune.

The solar system is about 4,600 million years old.

Planet	Average distance from Sun	
Mercury	35,960,000 miles	(57,910,000 kilometers)
Venus	67,190,000 miles	(108,200,000 kilometers)
Earth	92,900,000 miles	(149,600,000 kilometers)
Mars	141,550,000 miles	(227,940,000 kilometers)
Jupiter	483,340,000 miles	(778,330,000 kilometers)
Saturn	887,660,000 miles	(1,429,400,000 kilometers)
Uranus	1,782,880,000 miles	(2,870,990,000 kilometers)
Neptune	2,796,000,000 miles	(4,504,000,000 kilometers)

The name "solar system" comes from the word "Sol," the Latin name for the Sun.

On Saturn

As it travels around the Sun, the beautiful ringed planet Saturn spins on its **axis**.

Rotation and Revolution

Saturn **rotates** on its axis once every 10.66 Earth hours. Saturn does not spin in an upright position. Its axis is tilted over by 26.73 degrees.

Saturn is flattened at the **poles**. Its **diameter** from side to side is 74,853 miles (120,536 kilometers). However its diameter from top to bottom is only 67,520 miles (108,728 kilometers). This is probably because the substances in Saturn can move around very easily, and because Saturn spins very fast for such a large planet.

▶ Saturn is the most flattened of all the gas-giant planets.

8

Saturn orbits the Sun in 29.46 Earth years. This is Saturn's year. The orbit is almost a perfect circle. The Sun's gravity keeps Saturn revolving around it.

Saturn has seasons as it orbits the Sun, because its axis is tilted. Earth has seasons in the same way. However, there is very little difference between summer and winter on Saturn. It is not known why.

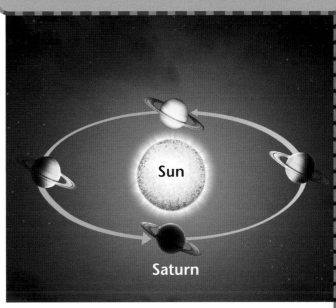

▲ Saturn's rings always point in the same direction as the planet revolves around the Sun.

▼ From Earth, the view of Saturn's rings changes.

From Earth, we see Saturn tilted in different ways, at different times of Saturn's year. This is because Saturn's tilted axis gives us different views of its rings. Sometimes we see them from above or below, and they show up well. At other times we see them side-on, and they seem to vanish.

Size and Structure

Saturn is the second largest planet. It is nearly 10 times wider than Earth. Saturn's diameter at the **equator** is 74,853 miles (120,536 kilometers). Its main rings are 169,000 miles (272,000 kilometers) from side to side, and less than half a mile (about 1 kilometer) thick.

Saturn is made up of about 75 percent hydrogen and 25 percent helium. There are also very small amounts of rock, and small amounts of the substances water, methane, sulfur, and ammonia.

Saturn is called a gas-giant planet because it does not have any solid ground to land on. The planets Jupiter, Uranus, and Neptune are also gas giants.

▲ Compare the size of Saturn and Earth.

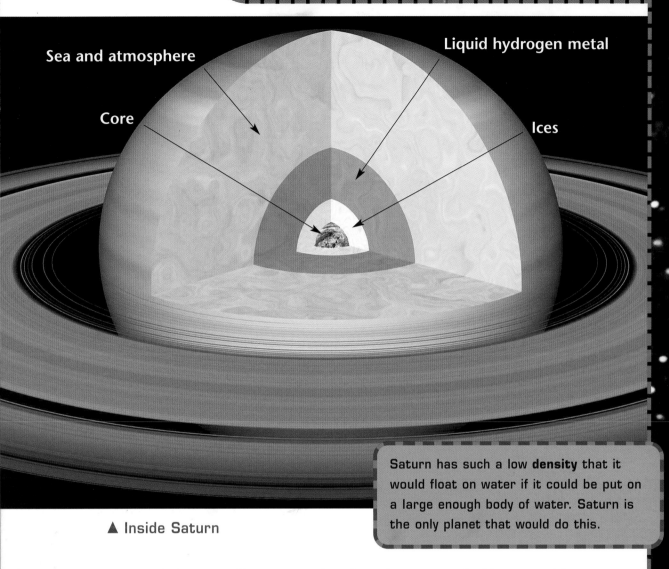

Sea and atmosphere

Liquid hydrogen metal

Core

Ices

Saturn has such a low **density** that it would float on water if it could be put on a large enough body of water. Saturn is the only planet that would do this.

▲ Inside Saturn

Saturn has a small **core** made of rock surrounded by ices. The core is probably about the size of Earth. There is a layer of liquid metal hydrogen around the icy core. Around the metal layer is a sea of liquid hydrogen. This hydrogen is not a metal. Above the sea is Saturn's **atmosphere**, a layer of gas which consists mainly of hydrogen and helium. Saturn's rings are made of pieces of rock and ice.

Saturn has a very low density, which means that it is very lightweight for its size.

11

Clouds

Saturn has bands of yellow and gold going around it. These colored bands are wider at the planet's equator than they are at the poles. The bands of color are clouds blowing around the planet. The clouds are made of **crystals** of ammonia, sulfur, and water drops.

Strong winds blow the bands of cloud around. The winds at the tops of the clouds can reach speeds of 1,100 miles (1,800 kilometers) per hour. Winds in the strongest hurricanes on Earth occasionally reach about 250 miles (400 kilometers) per hour.

▶ Saturn has cloud bands of yellow and gold.

Storms

The colored bands next to each other often blow in opposite directions. When they meet, there are storms with thunder and lightning. These storms can last for months or years. Some storms on Saturn show up as white oval shapes. In 1989, a red oval cloud was photographed which was similar to the Great Red Spot on Jupiter.

▲ The white arrow shape near Saturn's equator is a storm.

▼ Saturn has a red spot.

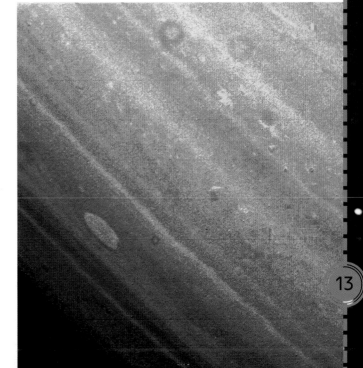

13

Making Heat

Saturn is warmer than would be expected of a planet that is so far from the Sun. It gives off more heat than it receives from the Sun, which means that Saturn must be making heat of its own.

Astronomers think that the substances inside Saturn are always being pushed tightly together. This would be caused by Saturn's strong gravity. The gravity pulls substances towards the middle of the planet. The particles would heat up as they are pushed up against each other, making the planet heat up.

Saturn also gives off more light than it receives from the Sun.

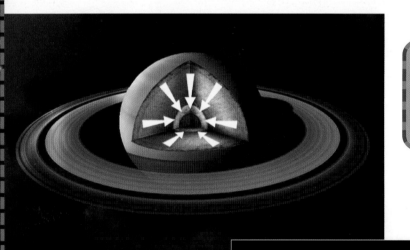

The heat that Saturn makes inside may help drive the very fast winds on Saturn.

▲ Inside Saturn, particles squeeze together.

▶ Heat is given off by Saturn

▲ An aurora on Saturn

Earth has auroras from time to time. They occur near the North and South poles. Auroras are curtains of white or colored light which hang in the sky.

Magnetic Field

Saturn has a strong **magnetic field** in parts of space around it. A magnetic field affects magnetic substances. (Earth also has a magnetic field.) Saturn's magnetic field is caused by the liquid hydrogen metal inside it. As Saturn spins, the hydrogen metal spins, making the magnetic field.

Saturn's magnetic field traps **charged** particles which have been floating in space. As Saturn and its magnetic field spin, these charged particles give off **radio signals.** These radio signals can be picked up from here on Earth. Saturn's magnetic field pulls down charged particles at the north and south poles. This makes **auroras** like we have on Earth.

15

Rings and Moons

Saturn has 56 moons circling around it, as well as thousands of rings of ice, dust, and rock.

Rings

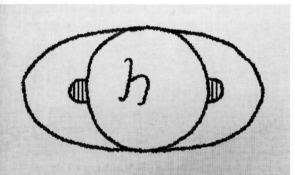

▲ Galileo's drawing of Saturn with "handles"

Galileo Galilei was the first person to look at Saturn with a telescope, in 1610. He was surprised to see that Saturn had two bulges, one on each side. He drew Saturn with two "handles." In 1659, Christiaan Huygens announced that the bulges were actually rings around Saturn.

Saturn's rings are very bright and are made of pieces of rock and ice. Most pieces are the size of dust, or up to half an inch (1 centimeter) across. Some pieces are several feet wide, even half a mile (1 kilometer) wide. Most pieces are probably made of water ice, and some pieces are probably rock covered with water ice. The ice makes the rings bright, as it reflects the sunlight.

Galileo Galilei was born in 1564 in Italy. He was probably the first person to study the Moon, stars, and planets with a telescope. He also invented the **thermometer**.

Saturn's main rings are about 169,000 miles (272,000 kilometers) across. This is the distance between the outside edges of the A ring, on opposite sides of Saturn. The rings are less than half a mile (about 1 kilometer) thick.

▲ Saturn's A, B, and C rings can be seen from Earth.

From Earth, we can see that Saturn has two obvious rings and one faint one. The obvious rings are called the A ring and the B ring. The faint one is known as the C ring. There is a gap between the A and B rings, called the Cassini division. There is another smaller gap in the outer part of the A ring, called the Encke division.

Saturn's rings are probably ice, dust, and rock which came from one or more moons which were smashed to pieces a long time ago. The rings are not solid—bright stars shine right through them.

Thousands of Rings

Space probes have visited Saturn and taken close-up pictures of the rings. These pictures show that Saturn really has thousands of rings. The rings are grouped together to make the rings named A, B, C, D, E, F, and G. The main rings of Saturn are the A, B, and C rings, going from the outside in. The space probes *Voyager 1* and *Voyager 2* discovered the faint rings which have been named D, E, F, and G.

▼ The rings of Saturn

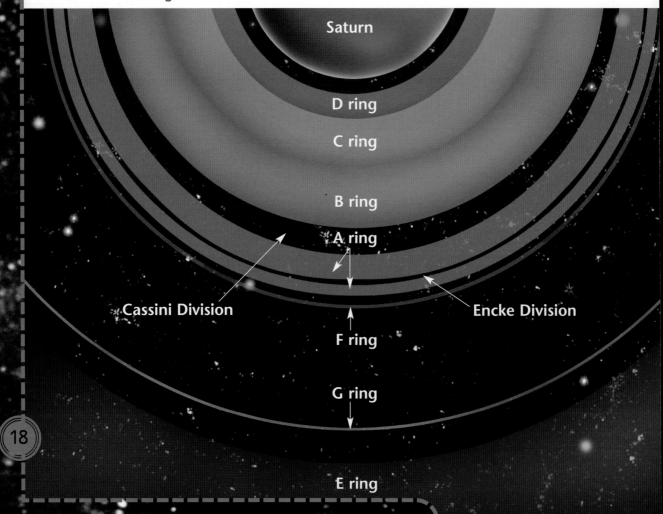

Saturn

D ring

C ring

B ring

A ring

Cassini Division

Encke Division

F ring

G ring

E ring

▼ This photo of the rings of Saturn was taken by the space probe *Voyager 1*.

- Saturn's D ring is inside the C ring. It reaches down to the cloud tops of Saturn.
- The F ring is just outside the A ring. The F ring is very thin and it is made of a few smaller rings. In some places, these rings are twisted together, making the F ring look a little like rope.
- The G ring is outside the F ring. It is even fainter than the F ring.
- The E ring is the very outside ring. It is very wide but very faint.

Moons

Names have been given to 35 of Saturn's moons. At least 21 more moons have been discovered, but they have not been given names. The Internet has up-to-date information on discoveries of moons—some Web sites are listed on page 30.

Saturn's 35 named moons include 8 larger moons and 27 smaller moons. All of the moons except one orbit Saturn outside the main rings that we see in pictures. The tiny moon called Pan orbits Saturn in the Encke division, which is a gap in the A ring.

One of Saturn's small moons, called Phoebe, is 8 million miles (13 million kilometers) from Saturn. It orbits in the opposite direction to the other moons.

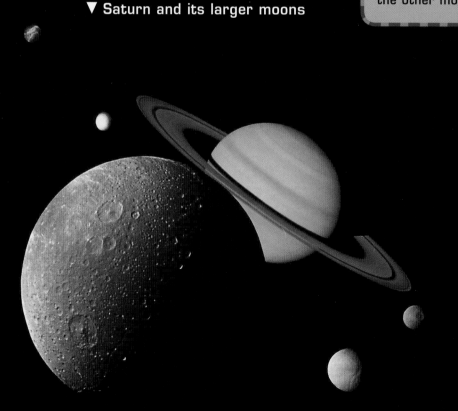

▼ Saturn and its larger moons

▲ Pandora

Shepherd Moons

Saturn has three small moons called shepherd moons. Shepherd moons help to keep Saturn's rings in place. They prevent the particles in the rings from flying out too far, or from falling in towards the planet.

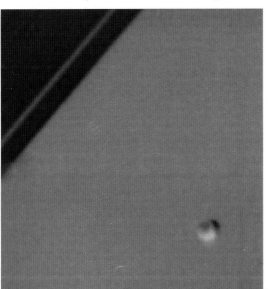

The tiny moon Atlas orbits Saturn just outside the A ring, keeping the A ring in place.

The F ring is kept in place by the small shepherd moons Prometheus, just inside it, and Pandora, just outside it.

◀ Prometheus

Titan

Saturn's largest moon is called Titan. It is the second largest moon in the solar system and is much larger than Saturn's other moons. It also looks very different from the other moons. Titan is probably made of rock and ice. Titan's diameter is 3,200 miles (5,150 kilometers)—a little larger than the planet Mercury.

Titan has a thick orange atmosphere around it which is full of haze and clouds. The atmosphere contains mainly nitrogen, as well as small amounts of methane and helium. Haze and clouds stop the surface of Titan from being seen.

▼ Titan

Titan's atmosphere may be similar to Earth's atmosphere when Earth was young. Astronomers might understand better how Earth developed by studying Titan.

Mimas

Mimas is the closest of the larger moons to Saturn. It lies at the beginning of the E ring. Mimas is made mostly of frozen water, with a small amount of rock.

Mimas has impact **craters** where asteroids have hit it. One huge crater, called Herschel, is about 80 miles (130 kilometers) across and has a mountain in the middle of it. Mimas would have nearly shattered into pieces when the asteroid that made Herschel hit.

▲ Mimas

▼ Enceladus

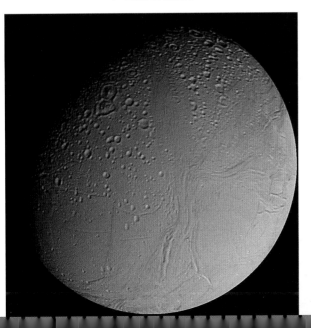

Enceladus

Enceladus lies in Saturn's E ring. It is the whitest large object in the solar system because it is covered in clean ice. Enceladus has some craters where asteroids have hit. It also has wispy streaks across it where the icy **crust** has cracked.

Tethys

Tethys lies in Saturn's E ring. It is made almost completely of frozen water. Tethys has one huge crater named Odysseus. Tethys must have been liquid or partly liquid when the asteroid that made Odysseus hit, otherwise Tethys would have shattered.

▶ Saturn, Tethys and Dione

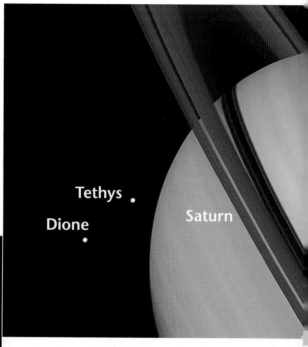

Dione

Dione lies just before the outside edge of Saturn's E ring. Dione is made mainly of frozen water. It has long, criss-crossing marks on one side where water has come through cracks in the crust and frozen.

◀ Dione

Hyperion

Hyperion is farther from
Saturn than Titan. Hyperion
is not round, but has an
irregular shape. Hyperion is
made mainly of frozen water,
however, it is dark in color,
so it must be covered with a
thin layer of dark substance.

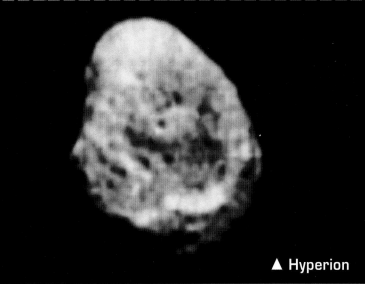

▲ Hyperion

▼ Rhea

Rhea

Rhea lies outside Saturn's
E ring. It is made mainly
of frozen water and
contains very small
amounts of rock. Rhea has
many craters on one side
and is smoother on the
other side.

Iapetus

Iapetus is the farthest large moon
from Saturn. It is made mainly of
frozen water. Iapetus is very bright
on one side and almost black on
the other side.

▲ Iapetus

Exploring Saturn

Saturn has been visited by a few spacecraft without any people on board. These spacecraft were operated by astronomers on Earth by sending and receiving radio signals. These types of spacecraft are called space probes.

The space probe *Pioneer 11* flew past Saturn in 1979. *Pioneer 11* took the first ever close-up pictures of Saturn, as it flew under Saturn's rings and over the cloud tops. It also made measurements of Saturn's magnetic field.

▲ An artist's impression of *Pioneer 11*

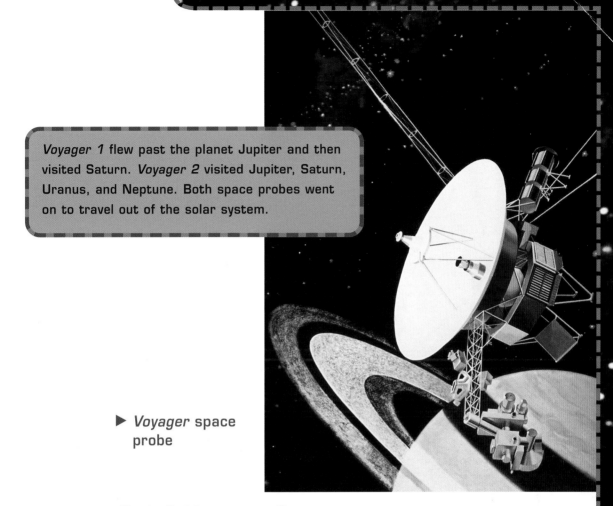

Voyager 1 flew past the planet Jupiter and then visited Saturn. *Voyager 2* visited Jupiter, Saturn, Uranus, and Neptune. Both space probes went on to travel out of the solar system.

▶ *Voyager* space probe

Voyager 1 and *Voyager 2*

The space probes *Voyager 1* and *Voyager 2* were sent to visit the gas-giant planets. *Voyager 1* flew past Saturn in 1980. *Voyager 2* visited Saturn in 1981.

The Voyagers took many close-up pictures of Saturn. The pictures showed many details in Saturn's clouds, such as swirls and oval storms, and revealed how the clouds move around the planet. The Voyagers found that Saturn's rings are made mainly of water ice. They discovered thin rings that cannot be seen from Earth, and twisted rings. The Voyagers also discovered some of Saturn's smaller moons.

◀ The *Hubble Space Telescope* above Earth

▶ Computer generated color picture of Saturn taken by the *Hubble Space Telescope*

Hubble Space Telescope

The *Hubble Space Telescope* (*HST*) is a telescope which orbits Earth, in space. It gets a clearer view of stars and planets than telescopes on Earth, because it is above Earth's atmosphere. The *HST* carries cameras and other instruments. It was sent into space on board the space shuttle *Discovery* in 1990. When *Discovery* reached space, the *HST* was released to orbit Earth on its own.

The *HST* has taken many excellent pictures of Saturn. In 1990, it photographed a huge white cloud near Saturn's equator and, in 1994, it found another white cloud. The *HST* detected auroras at Saturn's poles. It also discovered two of Saturn's smaller moons, in 1995.

Cassini space probe

The *Cassini* space probe arrived at Saturn in 2004. It is orbiting Saturn, observing the planet, its atmosphere, rings, magnetic field, and some of its moons. *Cassini* sent a probe called *Huygens* to Saturn's moon Titan.

Questions about Saturn

There is still a lot to learn about Saturn. One day, astronomers hope to find out the answers to questions such as these:

- How does Saturn make its own heat?
- How did Saturn get its rings? Why is it the only planet to have such bright rings?
- Are there liquids on Titan's surface?
- Why does Titan have a thick atmosphere?

◀ *Cassini* space probe

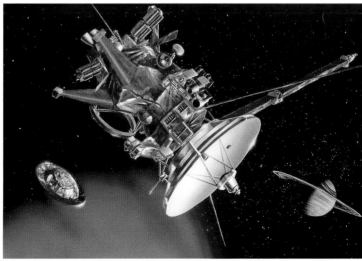

▲ An artist's impression of *Cassini* dropping *Huygens* into Titan's atmosphere

29

Saturn Fact Summary

Distance from Sun (average)	887,660,000 miles (1,429,400,000 kilometers)
Diameter (at equator)	74,853 miles (120,536 kilometers)
Mass	95.16 times Earth's mass
Density	0.7 times the density of water
Gravity	0.92 times Earth's gravity
Temperature (top of clouds)	–300 degrees Fahrenheit (–180 degrees Celsius)
Rotation on axis	10.66 Earth hours
Revolution	29.46 years
Number of moons	56 plus

Web Sites

pds-rings.seti.org/saturn
Saturn's ring system

www.nineplanets.org/
The eight planets—a tour of the solar system

www.enchantedlearning.com
Enchanted Learning Web site—click on "Astronomy"

stardate.org
Stargazing with the University of Texas McDonald Observatory

pds.jpl.nasa.gov/planets/welcome.htm
Images from NASA's planetary exploration program

Glossary

ancient from thousands of years ago

astronomer a person who studies stars, planets, and other bodies in space

atmosphere a layer of gas around a large body in space

auroras bands of light in the sky

axis an imaginary line through the middle of an object, from top to bottom

charged carrying electric energy

core the center, or middle part of a solar system body

craters bowl-shaped hollows in the ground

crust the outside layer

crystals tiny pieces of pure substance

density a measure of how heavy something is for its size

diameter the distance across

equator an imaginary line around the middle of a globe

gas a substance in which the particles are far apart, not solid or liquid

gravity a force which pulls one body towards another body

irregular not evenly shaped

magnetic field an area where magnetism occurs

mass a measure of how much substance is in something

moons natural bodies which circle around planets or other bodies

orbit *noun* the path a body takes when it moves around another body; *verb* to travel on a path around another body

planet a large, round body which circles the Sun, and does not share its orbit with other bodies (except its moons)

poles the top and bottom of a globe

radio signals invisible rays

revolve travel around another body

rotates spins

space probe an unmanned spacecraft

star a huge ball of glowing gas in space

telescope an instrument for making faraway objects look bigger and more detailed

thermometer an instrument for measuring temperature

trans-Neptunian objects small solar system bodies which orbit the Sun farther out than Neptune, on average

Index